Emma Lew | Crow College

Emma Lew

GIRAMONDO POETS

Crow College | New and Selected Poems

First published 2019
from the Writing and Society Research Centre
at Western Sydney University
by the Giramondo Publishing Company
PO Box 752
Artarmon NSW 1570 Australia
www.giramondopublishing.com

Designed by Harry Williamson
Typeset by Andrew Davies
in 10/16.5 pt Baskerville BT

Printed and bound by Ligare Book Printers
Distributed in Australia by NewSouth Books

A catalogue record for this
book is available from the
National Library of Australia.

ISBN: 978-1-925818-05-5

9 8 7 6 5 4 3 2 1

Also by Emma Lew

The Wild Reply

Anything the Landlord Touches

Nesselgesang (Germany)

Luminous Alias

For Abi and Francesca

And for Janet

Contents

New Poems

Introduction

Bella Li

Atmosphere, beyond the province of science, is an amorphous concept: difficult to define, impossible to convey with any precision. For these reasons, it is the most fitting appellation for the work of Emma Lew. Twenty years after the publication of her debut collection, *The Wild Reply*, the poems collected here, under the title *Crow College*, remain charged, pulsing with atmosphere. What does it mean to speak of atmosphere in poetry? It is to recognise the significance of the *sensed* over the *seen*; to be aware that a poetic use of language is constituted by the play between presence and absence, between what is revealed and withheld. Negative space, negative capability – in poetry these are cardinal qualities, and they are what give Lew's work its enduring power.

To read a poem by Emma Lew is to be led into an oblique narrative in which the beginning and end are unknown. Whether arriving with a theatre troupe on the heels of an army, mid-campaign, in 'Snow and Gold', or held 'in the fallow badinage of a ship's deck', months (or years) into a sea journey in the masterful and moving prose poem 'Bounty', we begin, time and again, *in medias res*. We are entering a cinema partway through a film, an auditorium in the second act of a play, a novel in the penultimate chapter. Images unreel before us, montage-like, giving tantalising glimpses of voices, landscapes, plots; the sense of a totality that escapes the frame.

The poems here primarily inhabit the dramatic mode: they deal in masks, artifice, impossible acts of witness; their personas are occupied by false memories, invented histories, fabricated impending or recent catastrophes. This is not to say they do not sound out biography or history, but that their central concerns are the chimera of the imagination. Ghosts, prophets, the ever-present dead, range through Old World Europe, post-revolutionary Russia, biblical and apocryphal scenes. Names mark familiar locations – Prague, Berchtesgaden, Chernobyl; each carrying their own heavy cargo of associations – but these are also not the places we know.

Hauntings feature prominently: from the possessed rural landscape of 'Marshes', where 'noon's/ ghosts are creeping across paddocks', to the uncanny domestic interior of 'Usual Rosettes', with its 'dour wallpaper/ always bulging at the seams', to the 'crowded rooms' of 'Freight', and its spare allusions to twentieth-century horrors. The restrained menace and sense of unease that runs like a live wire through many of these poems reminds us that the past recedes, but never disappears beneath the surface of the present. It troubles and it troubles.

Lew is a master of prosody: assonance, repetition and slant rhyme give poems such as 'Thebes', 'The Wild Reply', 'Nettle Song' and 'Falconer's Dawn' their complex, unsettling music. In later works, such as 'Anything the Landlord Touches' and 'Avalanches', Lew gravitates towards the pantoum: a traditional Malay verse form of cascading four-line stanzas, in which the second and fourth lines of one stanza become the first and third lines of the next. The pantoum is eminently suited to Lew's poetic strengths: it requires mastery of the single line, and a well-honed instinct for startling juxtaposition. In its circular movement, which takes us backwards as much as forwards, it is also a ghostly form – perpetuating a kind of sonic haunting, through echo and return.

Poetry, Emma Lew teaches us, is a condition of space through which something felt but unnamed works its way. Her poems are compelling precisely for their opacity, their 'luminous alias[es]'. They do what art is uniquely able to do: hold multiple stories, voices, threads of meaning. This precious ambiguity is the substance that rewards a reader not only on the first, but also the second, third, tenth reading. For those who have encountered Lew's poetry before, *Crow College* is a timely reminder of its undiminished power. For others, this will be an introduction to a vital and brilliant body of work unsurpassed in its ability to conjure whole worlds with the slightest and surest touch. This is a place to enter with lights out and senses sharp – 'Go with splendour into the blackouts'.

The Wild Reply

Procedure

Always turn to the usurer.
Start out and remain a villainess.
In the season of fake blossoms keep cool like the Minotaur,
talk proudly of elongated heads.

You will have to weaken for the month of December.
Maybe you'll quit thinking about soft rolling bones.
Take the silver away in your pockets.
Bring true fever to the classroom.

Go with splendour into the blackouts
and onwards for masonic nights.
Bide your time, then enter the slapping
while your bleak body still agitates.

Your dirty gloves jerk the grandeur
when smooth things meet, my dangerous clown.
Throw that veil of matchless colour:
it's what you do with vermilion.

How long must I wait for praise from a stranger?
At each séance I ask, *Is it good news?*
Keep the situation dark, let the tinsel linger –
that's how you'll create the universe.

Of Quite Another Order

When he came out of his forests
To figure in the literature of isolation
Or see if he could seduce mother-figures
As he had used to think (and be afraid) he could,
He was already the least curable, most diminished of people.
Civilisation increased his moments of sadness.
I knew this from the nature and number of scars:
Let them be collected. Let them be classed with method.

I would have given anything
To be able to make my pupil understand my act
And to tell him that the very pain of his bite
Could only delight me,
For that bite was an act of healthy vengeance.
He did not recover himself until he had reached the bottom of the stairs.
He used the word *berg* (mountain) to describe all things that are tall:
Let them be collected. Let them be classed with method.

He never leaves me without evident uneasiness,
So I took him to dine with me in the city.
I always talk to him in words that are part of a child's common vocabulary.
I'm struck by the splendour of his endlessly repeated motor gestures.
My education of the sense of sight being at an end,
I am to turn my attention to that of touch,
And later to myths of defeat:
Let them be collected. Let them be classed with method.

Afterlife

The whisper of a heavy car.
The darkness of trees and behind the darkness.
The pipe, the cool hills and the man.
Things you only buy once in a lifetime.

The shock of exile is wearing off.
Love celebrates its victory with two deaths.
I wanted to explain this to you in person,
knowing one day I will inherit your fortune.

I am large, I have a deep voice;
I broke the hands of my beloved.
The touchiest of giants, my theatre is promises;
my night is a continuous kung fu exercise.

A search and a shaking, the deep bows of etiquette.
White hoodlums; pure, senseless desire.
Close to the comfort of civil disturbance,
I find my composure equal to the hour.

So give, please, with speed.
Give until the colour black ends.
Make the matchbox do as it's told:
Just fire, no words!

In the Busy and Populous Belgium of Yesterday

In the busy and populous Belgium of yesterday
Doctors were going to their patients,
Weavers to their tapestries,
Children to their playgrounds.

But you were in a coma
And I was waiting for you to wake up.
Please don't confuse me by thanking me:
Your pride has cost us eleven days.

Always the same shapely volcano,
I could not react like an ordinary woman.
I was in the mood for ropes.
The sudden thaw saved me from my enemies.

And now, to celebrate our mistake,
Let us repeat it to ourselves again and again.
O let us begin with the bent arm of the standing man
Stuck in his terror.

You're agreeing to everything I say,
Hoping I'll go away.
And you can say 'maybe' all goddamn day –
But all this punishment isn't teaching me a thing.

Holes and Stars

I just got my memory back.
Few loons and I would live
in a corner at the airport,
not for the sequence
but the agony we had to be in,
running off with the money
and faking our own deaths.
Will technology make me remote?
I don't know where I am,
I never know what's going to happen.

Everything is quiet,
stunned yet animated,
evolving yet wilting.
If I want to read a newspaper,
I reach out for it with my hand.
Funny how you've taken my theory
and decided to call it your own.
They will be making snow tonight;
it will be beautiful and we can afford it.
Come quickly,
by yourself,
bring the negatives.

Alliance IV

You kissed me as tears welled in my eyes
Just before Christmas.

You came back and loved me unconsciously:
I refuse to pay for that.

I've written a strong but very dignified reply.
It simply says 'Lost'.

You cannot count on me for anything,
But suppose I volunteer to be harnessed?

As you know, I will be desperate
If that's the costume you want me to wear tonight.

Berchtesgaden

She tells a strange story of Hitler's love of astrology
She saw Goebbels with a red weal on his face
She says Hess is an addict of heroin
And says of Himmler *He still suffers from the effects of*
venereal disease contracted when he was only
a lad of twenty
Coarse Göring is always cracking jokes
Contrary to popular belief, the Führer is a late riser
Lunch is his favourite meal and begins with vegetable soup
He has a passion for trout served with butter sauce
Sweet potatoes usually accompany the fish
Sometimes an eagle is seen circling in the blue air
Guests assemble on the balcony before the dinner hour
Munich radio brings them *Die Lustige Witwe*
Rounded forms of crockery gleam in the great hall
The Führer's pockets are always filled with chocolates

They Flew Me in on the Concorde from Paris

They flew me in on the Concorde from Paris.
We were fortunate not to burn.
Over Shanghai I observed to my flautist husband,
'Such a metropolis needs a decent opera house.'
He rejected me in late May.
I resolved in future to express my feelings through my garden,
With an archway of zucchinis and cucumbers,
A bed of apothecary roses and high-yield grass seeds.

In the carpark at the Institute of Space Research
Women workers were performing their role of holding up half the sky,
While shipping companies complained about reserves of grain
Silting up the anchorage and all the sputnik could do was bleep.

I lodged with a senior government official in four elegant pavilions
Named after four seasons and bedecked with imitation sheep carcasses.
It was almost unthinkable not to give,
But I had no hard currency and could not afford contraceptives.
Thus I took a tonic in winter to be able to hunt tiger in spring.

I delivered my acceptance speech in the Great Hall of the People.
Citing the Scripture of Mountains and Seas,
I began by calling on steel makers to take up the way of Lamaism.
'Let's start calming down!' I cried.
'Let's get off painting and onto banking.
Differences are secondary to common interests,

They should not affect bilateral ties in a larger sense.'
I was applauded by reformists and conservatives alike.
Tell that to the lady in the morgue.
And tell her,
'When you get to heaven,
Maybe you'll get some answers.'

Chernobyl: Small Talk

I feel that I can trust you with a secret:
I've been ordered to fall in love with you
and I'm insanely worried about my eyes.
To this, add the collapse of my own
private world. I would kiss you
but am afraid to soil myself.

I'm inaudible. I'm babbling and my hands
are in a constant state of motion,
for love is immortal and lingers on
in dreams and waking visions. A fanatic
is not expected, but allow me to hanker.
Come over, the apples are ripe
in my guardian's orchards.

Something about the way you dance
reminds me that I have to sit down.
We are beautiful as long as we are masked,
and treachery is an affectionate game.
Like a circus, I cover my heartache.
Soon my mistakes will make me famous.

Caught in the Act of Admiring Myself

I love it when my doctor laughs in spite of himself
like we're equals.
The fact that he suggested I start
making medium-term plans
must mean he thinks I'm doing well,
because generally it's the better adjusted
who're up to making plans.
Consider,
he said,
working out
some aims professional/personal
and ways to achieve them –
a two-year/five-year plan.
But doctor,
I'm busy with the big nectarine in the fruit bowl
while the world plans around *me!*
Yes, and I sketched
a little gesture of doubt in the air
without moving my chin from my hand.

Message

I am over thirty
and have reached an age
to handle with care.

I don't listen
to songs of a peaceful reign
because I want to live, understand?
I want to take a look around.

When eating melons
I picture the athletes of my day
carved up like melons.
I like to see something for my money.

The credits come up and I roar.
The deluge begins and I hear flutes.
I can't live here,
these people are paste.

I have a wagon and I push it.
Why would I go to sea
where no one can admire me?

I'm Being Blackmailed Again

I'm being blackmailed again,
Cut off at last from my gains,
Bullied off the grieving seas,
Shut up on my own island.

Movement will help me to cope,
Crossing ten silent terrains
With the punishing, punishing, punishing
Features of my father.

You're trouble and you're expensive,
Everything you do fascinates me.
I've hidden the picture and prepared my alibi:
You'll never return from your holiday.

I hold particular views on pleasure,
In sharpness and strength finding opiates
To blur divisions between keeper and kept,
The backboned and the backbone-less.

This greed of mine has made my mind cunning,
The look of agony is only put on.
You mean no harm; it is done despite you,
Like water crumbling in a place of stones.

Multiple Kronstadts

What smooths the pliable into the mythical,
the icon into its frame?
What makes the sockets of the eyes
always those of the carver?

I don't mind your being a somnambulist,
bumping your head on all the hard walls
in the new shoes of the flat-footed
like the hanged, the gassed, the electrocuted.

I'm interested in the footprints you leave
in the mud Russians call 'roadlessness';
or are you coming by curtained car,
or by steamboat when the rivers are ice-free?

The more you shout about your strong nerves,
the more I want to fly in your air,
watching and not having to learn
the method of your wrecking hand.

Latecomer

There's been a curious agent doorknocking in the neighbourhood:
not a peddler, not a preacher, not a census-taker,
but a mild little man with lily hands and soft phrases.
They say that he's staking out Satan's lost ground
to swindle us of our eyes and souls...
That he's some raving escapee
loony in the solemn twilight...
That he's Mr Arnolfini and you can't put him off,
for he hazards his way in with insecticide breath
and leaves a card in cuneiform, in some weird script...
I believe he may pay a call at my house.
He'll enter, I do know, unclenching a valve
with feminine haunted arms.
I will start to dream in his dialect.
He'll teach me to shiver with a stranger purity.

Trench Music

There's an old heaven at work in me,
innocent as a cemetery.

It starts with the sound and speed of barricades,
more pillage and more homage.

Dancing with the bones of the lamb
near that delicate Stalingrad.

Entombed, bungled, fogged with breath;
naked never naked enough.

I cannot evade these forms in the bone,
the slow tunes from oblivion.

I fill up with shooting stars:
let my human half sing out.

The Way Out of Hungary

Our child must grow up in Paris
That yellow ochre and near-black light

I don't believe in the weakness of vanishing
The skeleton is the telling of a life

Please never be solemn with me
I love the facts you chant

The things we are supposed to know and feel and understand
There is so little to hide behind

We are always hounding ourselves
Why shouldn't we laugh, even if there is nothing?

My Adventurer

So I became his bluish-white partner.
Once during our courtship
He drew me into the room that housed
His personal archives and unlocked
That small collection of skeletons.
These, he whispered, would tell me
More than he was able to express.
Everything good comes from elsewhere, he said.

He showed me his warrior's real face.
A jousting lance had destroyed his other eye
And deep marks were scratched
By him with his own nail.
The incisions were always related,
In some obscure way,
To the thing that he was doing.
One must leave a trace and fix the memory, he said.

He recounted stories from a plague,
Explained the geometry of infinites,
Pairing with each thought its proper word.
Today everything goes in accordance with his wishes.
He has found a patron to finance the enterprise
And soon construction is to commence
On the pioneering railroad:
To run from Archangel to Murmansk, he says.

A pair of greyhounds lie in silent attendance
Like penitential saints upon our floor.
I am neither standing nor kneeling,
Gently tilting my perfected head at subtle angles.
And the gesture I make is centuries old.
Often have we sat like this,
His questions are still the delight of my world.
But they are imperfect, he says.

Accountancy

A man invited me to wrestle,
just a man with a normal heart.
That same commissionaire
set the forest alight.

The sky's blue was defeated
by his vision of little corners,
and the half-mad were mingled
wild in the radishes.

Summer could at any moment
end the jugglings of the wolves.
A midnight breeze rips the strings,
then the water attracts us and we dive.

More than once he falls down in the street
in the most calming way I've ever seen.
He always falls like a moody angel –
it's what he means by 'the plan of things'.

Aubade

Dawn's massing her old bully self
Above us in a lurid mood,
Her order gone to wrack in a day.
She'll soon put things to sordid rights –
Methodically lick out street lights,
Scuttle cross-dressers from the soiree,
Strain night sweats into resealable vials.
But I don't know that I can behave;
That I won't pull some Taurus effrontery,
When all she offers I've no heart for:
Newlyweds, the dead in them;
War crying, *Wage me! Wage me!*
Orphanages of ideas.
I feel, here on your tranquil shoulder,
Safe from her – your trigger finger
Lays me out on our prairie bed.

Earlier Cartographers of the Moon

You understood aether,
but problems crowd in on morning
and you can no more trick
the universe into granting favours
than your parents into loving you.

Soon you open a window and shut a door,
learning two of life's great lessons.
A lock and a key –
and civilisation is creeping in,
melting metal for a peal of bells.

Eerily managed reality
has made your life-work fragmentary,
so put the energy of sunlight in your mouth
and come out of observatories without a word:
we are not free to tell our dreams.

Little Sister

Smile at me like you smile at police,
Steady this shiver place a bit.
The evening is acting up and yelling half-rhymes.

Who hectors at the door?
Who, which bastard beautiful bastard
Comes tempt me?

See me seek heat
See me be flung
See me and say she is
Beauty of Prague before the War.

Do spies love, Em?
What is left of our family
Must make do on cold philanthropy.

Will we, by summer, be improved;
Check out of mercy hospital,
Take an ocean cruise?

How Like You

How like you, cholera,
to worry over the health of strangers.
And you have let your sweetheart go hungry,
while your legend crossed the country,

a surprise visitor playing Cupid,
keeping the happy happy –
from guest wing to portrait gallery,
prickly wilderness to deepest city.

With a grace of Goth and Hun,
you taught the danger of your good turn –
in roadless times, with early spoons,
and it only took an afternoon.

You rise like Islam this mauve morning,
inventing dark and savage deserts.
Tonight you launch them from the spire
and they'll spread like spiny fire.

Bungalows

I wanted a name that didn't have dark or death,
and the name of silver made me very cool:
a handful between bad and worse,
the tamed minutely beautiful.

Anything but Indian Lake,
where the syringe has pride of place
and pays for the journey but leaves nothing over;
yet I go there by bus with a suitcase.

I have seen a girl weep nightly
over her geometry,
driven to the violin
by simple opium.

Whole faces disappear into bandages,
bound hands make it a mystery.
In de facto asylums
the disciplines are talking.

I'm looking forward to small amounts,
demons have pushed me again.
They lie all night in one of my arms,
which is a creeper called the blue vine.

Thebes

I think of you as you are
at noon. One cloud in
a clear sky, oh that
one cloud! Your days
are like smoke, wild
as prophets. Fruit fallen,
throats to the dagger.

A dead language in
the blood. A fury locked
in the body crepuscular.
Ghost town, torn and
white. All I ask you
to do is radiate.

Stormlight and the
coming-on of night.
Moan of planets, mice
on the path. The dark
charge of doors and
the lake that burns.
Every method of howl
shaping the swoon.

The Wild Reply

I must not touch fire
Myth fire, adder's fire
Sensual and deaf
The deep, swift fire

Why do I dream?
Flame speaks and sings
The great barn burns
Mirage creeps in

I need proofs, not flame
The false weight of flame
I mean by this fire
King, give me fire

The smelting and the forging
I have flame and lack nothing
Beast in my footsteps
Light up, burn

The seed and the spark
The first flame of love
There is no fire
But the poems are beautiful

The Recidivist

There's a long-subdued fire bursting
in my erotic medicine chest;
the moon in its bruise and limping fiends,
and flesh from the palm of the hand I lost.

I've always loved the haunted moment
when night refills with fresh blood;
and dark bare death's speaking human words:
I've done it. I do it. I'll do it again.

Atoning dust blows here every day,
ancient sunlight cools my sins.
Get me out of here, there's a shortage of coffins
in this bitter hemisphere.

Anything the Landlord Touches

The Tale of Dark Louise

Must there always be some stray, hungry suitor?
I strive and I struggle, I can't keep the wolf.
On the day foretold by the travelling scholar,
I take my hank of flax and ride out.
The herring in the sea fall into a trance.
I put on the dress that brought me this shame.
Fire is never out of my chamber,
and the convent's interdiction falls between.
I'm not beautiful, but my eyes are drunk with music.
I will write whatever I want on your soul.
The vine is heavy again with the sweetest grapes,
and the ale flows, and the cellar drowns.

Marshes

They speak of stridency and of nothingness
and wrap up their shoulders in grey light.
I want to walk again in this miry place.
I want the fever and fret beneath, though
it's something I forget, like pain.

Sky a tent immaculately pitched and noon's
ghosts are creeping across paddocks.
Low, lame winds grow in the rushes –
the smoky pool mad in its sleep. I have
found earth still adhering. I wait for storms
to crack the glamour open.

I don't know the language of this country.
It begins in mists, sombre wild bees.
Moss sophistry while I lie listening. Dark
snake rumours grave in my ear.

Butterflies edged with wonder. Sly harrier,
cool stealing the day. A wraith's day –
slow and gentle and ravaged. This whole
calm world's sweet venom. My puritan
soul half in a sea, clawing deep in the peace
of mud.

Falconer's Dawn

What is the motive of light?
Birds rise like night from the soil,
beautiful wing-made murmur fading,
the intake of breath
so slight and slurred.

From my maps
the lake is nameless.
The moon seems too heavy,
stumbling in cloud.
Birds have moved into my arms
and are flourishing.
The glistening, brittle
world is mine.

Birds fly as the threnody pours.
Let them come twice
past my outstretched hand.
Let them tangle and list
and submerge
as day throws down
its berries and pearl.

Perhaps the Travellers

Not the most remarkable things but the things
nobody has ever seen. We went ashore on barges
in the mid-morning or flopped in the streets
of perfectly ordinary villages. June, almost dawn,
after the valley. We spoke in French, of course.
I did not forget to limp; and when it was cold
in my room I wrote there, the visible passages
letting down the grey light, so that when
he asked whether I was in pain, I said, 'No';
and sometimes, when I confessed, and I said
that I had nothing to confess, my conscience
was arrows. This is the beauty of effacement.
It happened so often, and for so long, that I became
someone else – a promise akin to breathing,
secreting myself in other people's ruined lives,
as dusk came poor across the river, shimmering
over the ancient houses, like the forms
of precious vessels, having no wound to feign.

Her Embroideries

He was the shadow of the deep bed.
He was very beautiful and, as always,
there was something perfect,
as though I were his cousin.
On the map he had shown me
a forest, but there was no such forest,
hence the lies, the discomfiture,
and the rest – the manor, steeped
in the odours of freshly ploughed
earth; shops rife with Trieste dialect.
And his messages ended with vows
like, 'Believe me, I am always
at your side.' It is impossible
to relate what or how he played,
the sudden modulations that
I could not grasp. I felt at such times
that only my body was riding,
yet I said the loveliest things.
He awoke with the violence
of the sensation, so that I was forced
to fasten with pins. His sisters again
donned their sombre mourning.
Even the sea birds lost their way.
And then the moon rose and shed
a different light. Listen – how he
dreams, how he weeps!

Rose Constructions

Sometimes my teacher
changes her conduct strangely,
pressing her heart
like dead leaves.
She sleeps in the chapel,
which is haunted.
Already the shadows
write in her diary.

She burns the letters
silently, reverently.
Like a bride,
she pushes away her plate.
She reads to me
like a will-o'-the-wisp,
and I ask her
if there are bitter drops
in everyone's cup.

She says, 'I respond
to the ploughing
of the fields,
whereas a man
grows fainter by a love.'

All the things
we talk about
I sew into the seams.
She opens the window
and lets in the dark flowers.

Nettle Song

Why glimmer? Seize fire!
What has sunk? The sweet hour,
all havens, the corners –
gloom's in the folds!

The rose has broken,
I am in fever.
Lead me to hyacinths,
let me run to seed.

What's in your heart?
Glaciers, glaciers,
a strange, cruel starvation,
the smallest storm.

What are your riches?
Puddles and thistles,
Burst fruit, such ashes,
wild as I wish.

Shoes of the Morning Star

He moved the sky and the sea's identity,
and from the forest came harshness.
He knew the scatter of all blown leaves,
the multiple small shadows. He needed
grandeur on the outward journey,
and his aspirations – a slip of moon,
the most broken trees. The low horizon
struck as a child. Echo came to him
from the shut-in town. It was like a rain,
the world, and his eyes loved faint things.

Snow and Gold

So, on the heels of the army, our troupe moved.
I gave birth in the street and night nailed the great city to the earth.
I saw the plague stalking like a stranger whose language I could not
understand.
My sores were dressed, my handkerchiefs hemmed.

It is one thing to listen to the heart and its murmurs.
A strange woman came to see me, saying that she was my lover's wife.
It was the twilight hour that is called the 'grey hour', when mourners
become lost and follow the wrong coffin.
We walked a little way together, and the talk burned like agate.

I know they say that one should speak well of the dead or not speak
at all.
The winter came in one jump like the wolf.
An eye grew sightless because there were frightening scenes I did not
wish to see.
I had talent for the noble virtues of blind faith even then.

An agile acrobat threw his plank across the ditch.
The wine now travelled from mouth to mouth.
The sentry's face clouded over, and he wept at the prompting of my
fingers on the strings.
So the young men paid their precious francs.

The wagons pulled out to the east like a sunburst.
Of course I sang, like a log covered with ice.
We lived unbuttoned through the black country,
taking such great mouthfuls of bread, as though we were seagulls.

What was I besides the strength of my shadow?
I climbed up on the trains and tossed down coal.
The wind blew and merged with me, my childhood and my life,
    my passions and transgressions.
Even if they weren't gold, the trinkets glittered.

I often wonder how unpenitent people could live under a sky.
It was that kind of Tatyana I had come to be.
Let my father say as many harsh and stupid things as he likes,
but the skin of my hands was like fine snow.

Bounty

These precious months have been like the withered rose. I say to myself often that I am now suffering. Absence binds us, and in the fallow badinage of a ship's deck, my former calm and piety are returning. O my darling, the rigging swarms. Help me out of this blind life. The shouts of gulls, the groping reefs. Our ship, with its great iron heart. Yesterday I had so much faith, I would have given half as much again to stray. In a sort of reverie I heard your voice, and I left everything and came like a star. My thoughts are churned by a thousand fins. I do worship, but I must not fall down. I have sometimes closed my eyes to what I see, for I know. What right have I to dictate to the wind? I ramble in the breast of a storm. I am alone and I have no chain. Black fathoms adorn the sailor, depths shine with insistent light. Strange grandeur shuts me in, and the way I move, so wrong in each limb. The sea has made a mouth of itself, like a huge man capable of the most delicate phrases. *Religion is revolution estranged*, it's saying in its own wild language. Geology teaches that death was in the world. Night by night the chant is borne. The waves make a senseless pillow. It is nothing here but bare and the hardest light from early dawn. O my darling, the gale has wreaked. I give you the feel of grey over ocean, and its crumpled face has mystery, in the wind's making and dissolving.

Famous Vexations

I loved the penitent's average face.
At the corner of every street,
beating rain.
I was pushed towards evil
in my most beautiful attire.
In searching for faith,
I soiled my hands.

Water, wind, morning.
It is fragrant.
Just think, I again dream.
All words become pale.
There are treasures to be taken
away from this country.
The palette darkens.
Here is my plan.

Kind of a Golden Girl

Kind of a golden girl, living that wonderful life
Some idea of midnight falling prey
Completely alive, not saving myself
Ces petites misères qui gâchent notre vie

Some idea of midnight falling prey
I did everything I could to be that shadow
Ces petites misères qui gâchent notre vie
With their promises of heaven, and their hands

I did everything I could to be that shadow
The brotherhoods do tear apart
With their promises of heaven, and their hands
I take the harsh things, poor twilight work

The brotherhoods do tear apart
What you touch is my false history
I take the harsh things, poor twilight work
As if I could get back into my own mirrors

What you touch is my false history
Completely alive, not saving myself
As if I could get back into my own mirrors
Kind of a golden girl, living that wonderful life

Pursuit

I have not had fortune but I have seen the resplendent moths
of Daghestan. I have travelled through clusters of their castles
and found them wingless, lain deep, like the oak apple.
And in Angola I have seen hundreds of butterflies grieving.
I have seen butterflies swerve like the fiddle and the bow.
I once heard a boy sing on the deck of a Black Sea steamer,
There is a small and fragile bug!

The respiration,
the pulses of the heart, the beating that bursts the lid of the shell.
In Sago I found the weevil itself, and I smelled the perfumes
of the males. Often I've dreamt of the wasp's tumbled journey,
the mosquito's guilt and thrift, how the ant slipped down
to haunt the grass, how the hornet left only the skin of my fruit.
For insects have a beauty that hurts, and that may even darken
the sky. They drum with their bellies upon the twig. They have
learned to cleanse their blood with light. I have seen a mantis
of a delicate mauve impaled on the flea's single spine. I have
known the mere segmented grub, and I have shared the earth
with lice. In the forests of the Congo, I recorded the stickiness
of swarms. O unforgettable flies of Palestine! O cicadas of Spain
in the year I was born!

Usual Rosettes

Once, twice. Today, tomorrow. There will always be a limit.

MARC CHAGALL

Early flowers caused the frost, but the plane tree
threw its shadow, and the lilac bush stood cool,
shocking the house like fresh linen. My father
supported my mother in such precautions.
They quarrelled and broke, no matter how
it simplified things, and her large white skin
was smooth – sweet though forbidden. I could
make a lake of the dusty bundles that held
everything in life for me – the dour wallpaper
always bulging at the seams, the kitchen
cupboards of pine without knots, the hurled
unbreakable plates on the floor. The street below
had just begun to heal. Strange to come away
from the lamplight, the knife grinders calling out,
deafening the empire. I loved the fireworks,
but I needed to be saved from myself. Cracks
demoralised our little house. Father surfaced again
when the fortune was lost, and mother rained
into every room, proudly hampering herself
while we ate a dark soup. Yes, in the past
everything is beautiful, like a twilight where
water would flow very slowly – the chastenings,

the bread, the pallor; the fires I started
so they could not see me cry. I played a game
called 'Wreck Everything', though I dressed
in silks and delicately nurtured thanks.
But now I'm frightened of another sort of ruin,
and the orioles nest someplace else.

Particulars

She stepped on me symbolically
by stepping on my coat.

Her general air
was one of melancholy
and lassitude.

My interest was in part aroused
by so cruel a desertion and so strange a fate.

She expressed the desire
to be 'herself ' again.

She spoke of vague apprehensions,
a strong compulsion
to break all the china upon the table.

The least noise made her start.
I asked if she felt haunted by futility,
and she wept, and agreed.

I passed the day with her in conversation
in this very room,
forbidding entry to all my servants.

We sat in comfortable armchairs facing each other.
Outside the wind was causing the leaves to drop and die.

In the dream she had dirtied her knees.
We examined what was revealed,
what concealed,
to and from whom.

At one point I became aware
that she was animating her hands,
as if to craft the twilight into some tangible form.

Jasmine

Breaking off a thread newly woven,
she falls silent. Her fear: that the dead
will jump up to settle accounts.
Little showers? Hail? She understands
this completely. So many thieves
wandering in the house. 'The black wind.
Do you hear?' ask the ghosts.
Her family is quicksand in such rooms.
All day she has felt uneasy
about the letter in her pocket.
Shame on her, in the setting sun.
See? She is lost. She's left the hours
in that house and now she tastes nothing.
The moon happily displays its scars.
The only path has been blocked –
who can forget that? And someone
is making trouble by the well.

The Stopping Place

Darkness tied up the bells of our troikas.
It snowed a little in the night and in the broth.
Tender love and then the iron. The mastiff,
off her leash. The violent widow also came
to nothing. Yet the stain: it was as if the silence
could do no harm. And the Heir Apparent
was obviously burning. What if they had come
and started rifling through our things,
and found silhouettes?

Fast

She believed every dumb line she ever had to say.
She swanned in voluminous crinoline,
her marred eyes seeming to wish more to veil.
Perhaps the darker tresses were a cry to the world,
but there was a larceny in her too,
a jittery jumping-off and onto.
Some part of her would always be twitching,
and she'd break up long words
because she liked the air moving.
There are women who breathe only in the lair of spies.
Savageness moulds their laughter.
Svelte in the weeds behind the porch,
she slayed her men with a husky voice,
and the swirling leaves casually brushed her body.

Loquax Ludi

What will memory do to us?
We loved the nights and were taken,
all in our velvet dresses, to grind
stardom down to its dusty elements.
Or worse, the way we moved,
flashing like trout. We were nymphs
trespassing in the twiggy depths,
and the certainty that we would float
was absolute.

How we trampled upon the thing
that haunts! We could be at sea,
then back with unseen ferocity, our
greedy great mouths full of thees
and thous. This is our story –
very pink, very gilt and grandiose.
Young men had lilies in their wooing,
all locks to thieves gently unbound.
And our highest hopes – to live
as softly hummed, to hammer
wisdom through the walls, to be
lulled by walk and endless sun.

Thirty Versts

The miracles are not mine

GRIGORI RASPUTIN

When you asked me if I wanted to ride,
I said that I did not know, because I wanted to
but I was afraid of you. And so the summer
passed like breath, and this feeling
has prevailed above all others.

The procession on the streets with the carpet
and the candles. This monogram I have
stamped on the paper with a thing.
The oddly shaped eyes of the stately women.
Your power was tremendous, it was like dust.

The night can touch something of yours.
I am the boldest of the sisters. The string broke,
the pearls scattered on the floor. Others say
that I was ordered to leave for the provinces.

We are all tempted in this world, and we repent.
I am fasting, trying to attain. Danger lengthening
in the city. Dominoes in the evening
with the wind.

We live here on earth but we are already
half gone: how shameful and how terrifying.
I wear your cross on my grey tea gown.
Even in our house the child was born suffering.

But the Irtysh is long since frozen over,
the imagination is clear and impure.
I have no fever, which baffles and angers.
A light which drives my thoughts towards rain.

Sinking Song

You, me, money and fear –
the rings of planets through our hands.
We are just strong enough
to make the tides work for us.
We could move in the veins of orchids.

In the wonderful phrasing of this evening,
fire runs along us as a man.
All vanished animals weep,
and cities, built merely to fall,
drown in birds.

Come, trust the world – it's still night,
and the moon wishes to dissipate,
and earth groans under its weight of mice,
and God has given us everything,
everything.

The True Dark Town

The snows were melting but I wanted to speak.
Swollen and undressed, filling the roads.
The mountain, so beautiful. We were afraid.
    Death buttoned my coat.

I smelled their odour when they came
down the incoherent paths of the mountain.
The petals of the flower were hushed.
    It's the blood from that night.

A child has sheltered her books with her body.
A man was seen hoarding. Who can be sure?
This is the only thing I have rescued.
    It's pitiful.

When the rain came, when they opened fire.
Such trifles as the noise of stars.
I had no idea the dead were so heavy.
    It's autumn now.

The past will be a bitter land.
I do not trust the face of my father.
The wind, they say, is going to blow till the end.
    The fleas are hungry.

Red

Find some truly hard people

LENIN

Leagues apart, and in what latitudes together,
in the most forlorn regions of the oceanic city,
and here moving softly through the listening crowd,
we came and we came, and we left our machines
at night, and everywhere hidden wires had only
to be touched. Class hatred had then just dawned.
Cables of denial sped. I remember how the tolling
of a bell would flood, the insurrection surely
cutting my face. Some high official was thrown
into the river, and this became the meshing
of the wheels, and when lightning struck that part
of the old palace, all the theatres were deceived,
or deceived themselves. We were the hired
and the depraved, thin and dark and unjust,
prepared to burst in that ray of light when it came,
hearing nothing and scribbling until the stupid lamp
began to smoke. Every day we had to thieve
and dive and take the lifted hand of destiny
for a dream. The mud seemed a merciful provision,
the village did its best to teach us fear. Or was it
the darkness of expectation and secret emissaries
who had come the same way? We were shadowy
in our own eyes as well, denouncing only

when silence failed. Depots, arsenals – we could
dare those raids with new extremes of shivering
force, and death was just a tremor far down,
the master who lies in the heart of the serf.
What we were whispering became the clamour,
so the cargo of the ship was unseen and not
thought of, and we had been carrying
impeccable papers, fine ardour among us
on our straight path. My wound sparkles
at these memories: how victory was so often
a collapse, how the pines ran past our sledges
like soldiers, and the wind was always pressing
on the earth. The very themes were existence
and did not dissolve, for the true mind does not
need a body for its life, like the bombs, which
we knew must come, spoiling the small pleasures
they dispensed.

Light Tasks

I arrived in bits,
furious at Copenhagen.
The swans were stretching their necks and biting.
The donkeys stumbled badly on the descent.

How nice your compliments sounded –
it was as if the lights in the priory hall
had been turned on all at once.
The cabbage was marvellous.
Oh! If only I were dressed better!

You seemed a little wanton.
Thistledown, someone said.
And all were weeping, men with white beards.
The dog had perhaps been noble and faithful.

Thousands of pineapples came
by steamer.
The policemen on the streets gave directions
in the most attentive fashion.
The church arches were splendid,
the pillars slender,
and when we were walking on the road
you wrote the word *changelessness* in the sand with your foot.

My mind was like an angel sinking.
Among the ruins of four walls you showed me the sea –
how it and the starry sky were constructed.
It was ebbtide. I undressed.
How many hearses in the coming year?

The children herding cows were so beautiful.
One questioned me about the darkness.
Ships with all their sails, I said.
All the melodies of pain at every shift,
and then the endless moon, growing and growing.

Passage

Papa may have ceased his wanderings
My country is this small plain between rain and wind
Behind the scrawls is a burning
Small towns, clean, with a church
Streaked moon, the crop is rusting
I am coming to life at last

The movements of horses kept well in hand
The suddenness that speaks of a leap
The many trains I have taken
To be drowned in rags like this
He has no house, only a key
The terrible carved-deep grief

In the digging-down perfection of night
No animal seems like the wind
The human hardness of a jewel
The shine and shadow of the skin
Blind echoes of us in stone
When will I hold all this in my hands?

Praise Report

We are on holy ground and I take off
my shoes, and I'm crying my own
real tears, and that sunny faith
I've been searching I've been seeking,
and I know for sure love is blind
because He says

Say that a man makes a vow and
lives it, and he comes a long way
and now he falls, right in front of God
and everybody, and fires will burn
and that you know

I confessed my sins and they are under
the blood, and I sinned back then
when I was caught behind my shadow,
and I confess it to you and I confess it
to the Lord, and I'm driving down
the road, I'm praying

It may be that I am harbouring in
my heart, walking in evil, walking
in the ways, my God says He gives me
the fires, God chose the weak things
of the world to shame

Plantain

For he comes, the human child

W.B. YEATS

The third night you reached out to me
in your sleep, like this.
Alive with trees, when you met your father.
Thinking that we were somehow becoming
invisible to God. Be sad
about some of the things that are here.

Now they have planes to spray the fields.
I think they even have machines
to cut the bananas from the trees.
No telephone to ring up on and say,
'My baby has been born.'
The night you climbed crying into,
like a story, with no hurry.

I want to rise close in your heart.
I have named you and feared.
Small openings in the walls
and the heat in dark spaces.
It is as if you had emptied all the jars.
And I struggle: where are my pieces?

Everything is the night that tears.
I know this region's profit.
A black snake circling on itself.
The jungle, growing very high.
I wanted to look at the moon
in your fingers, as if to say,
'I've chosen.'

My Illusion of the Tycoon

1

Genitals once appeared in a letter he sent me,
and gray wool so that I might be seen in company
with him. He was elaborately courteous,
and stood alone like music. Even desire
includes a kind of mourning.

2

I struggled with my other lens, sometimes
aiming at the camera behind the eye.
The nakedness is always his. Each pointless
ornament is loved. He saw my pictures,
he walked at night, up the paved street,
into the arms of barren elms.

3

Long emulsions and tiny aperture.
The dressing-for-dinner, the exact stallions.
Warm enough for the modernist deck chairs,
and guests were seen moving among the statues,
where he had dreamed. It was jazz,
but very languid jazz, although he himself
danced with some abandon.

4

A shot I took, probably in October.
Man yearning over marble, and gradual alcohol.
The ferry and its schedule; the dog, huddling.
Sun on a straw hat next to the stair.
That day the youngish woman in the market.
The sea, rumpled by a wind and slow need.

5

The gesture, the expression, and of course
the magnificent devastation – these
are images of surrender we do not know.
He had admitted me into his room,
closing the moment when light elopes.
Dangerousness of the man, it is quite beautiful.

6

Screens, mirrors, artifice – I assemble him.
What haunts is the absence the eye collects.
The photograph accepts the dark truth.
His puzzling home, his imperfectly knotted tie,
and Chinese rain today at last.

Riot Eve

I haven't, thank God, become a perpetrator.
I never caused the death of others, though I must utter these words.
I hold myself back, as the shrewd son of my father.
I see it like this: a lion will attack a gazelle.

We have one life. Why spend it being feebly decent?
We see but one night; we contain others.
I ask myself if this path and all those terrible detours were really necessary.
There is a reason for everything, and our catastrophe.

Imagine then that a father returns and doesn't speak about any of this.
He carries me on his shoulders during the long walk in the forest.
Imagine a man – so polite, so clean;
his swiftness, his warmth, his murderous ideas.

Look, nothing in this world is perfect.
This is the condition, now growing darker.
History has shown us: the Black Death, the Borgias...
I await the real wooden anger that shapes me.

The gardens have roared for days.
The wind bends the trees. It is like a sign.
I hear of a palace rising.
It is just after midnight, and I will obey you.

The End of Debonair

He moved like a panther
and his price was right.
I got married perilously close,
laughing at the notion
of another's lust.
Think fast, now.
Think fast.

OK, strip the glacial
femininity to bone truth.
No water in the pool,
but he'll die young.
'Would a little malice
be so undesirable?'
Anything to get him
hand-to-mouth.

Never,
even in my wildest.
Knowing I'd be
getting in his veins.
Nothing with the heart
is ever just a little.
'Fall apart in my hands,
I still have hopes.'

Man Coming Back as a Bird

In the office he unfolded the papers.
Other times I saw him press his pencil
harder, and still no sense. We were watching,
I thought, a man tapping on windows,
too much in love with his ink and spit.
Genius who made night in his little room,
he drove himself from rain to hail,
with his rigid thanks ('there is something
wrong with me'), wounding himself
where the buses go up the street.
I don't know for sure why he had
such a hard time with words,
why he clenched his fists and went forth
to the midnight feast as if to crumbs.
I felt great fear for him in the barren fields.
I couldn't have found a plain limb to touch.
What country did he mean: 'shining
in its illness'? I think he saw a moment
when he could fly up emerald, make
his mark – as if his axes cut down nothing,
as if he had been crossing bridges all his life.

Flourish

I never bet on melancholy
There's parish in the spittle of an angry man
Fame is the shell which preserves that thunder
The late bloomer has become the talk of the town
Truth is a jewel to avoid
I'll show you a relic equally holy
A beautiful plan, where everyone ends up happy and rich
What I want is to get this pain off my body
Irony is the rage that fails
Look at me: I'm blind, I'm living a wonderful life
I rise early and take the hazardous road
The curse has fallen on me too, but in reverse

Prey

I was daydreaming about wiping out the whole school
I was rehearsing and perfecting the 'gentle giant' approach
Rebellious and defiant, had no ambition
Death is a beginning, it's beautiful

I swore I never shot at a windowless wall
I was calm and denied, and was allowed to drive away
And killed a young bride, inconclusively
It's sad, but I don't live there any more

Not like you'd expect – real dark, red blood
Humid in the city known for its beer
I was wrestling with a list, perhaps posing as a cop
And I wrapped my fingers around your throat. Did you panic?

I'm not an expert, I don't know the terminology
They were looking for a guy who was ghoulish or foamed
It's a slow road with a lot of curves
Maybe I should have toyed with her more

Sheraton Evening

I am a businessman –
not a dissident any more,
moulting into my cup
in the lobby by the fern,

they all struggling after their gods.
Then night congeals and sorts out
those who have eaten from
those who are about to dine.

Less spare heart space –
how to define this desire
before retiring to my suite
to lie lung up in my last bath?

Here's how:
The river runs both ways.
The world does move.
For a ten-horse sacrifice
it blows your hair back.

Storm

What a wild heretical light
when day bursts its filmy skin,
and pain's already in the wind,
and the sun sees itself
shattered into air,
and thunder
shivers down,
so frail now
in the lost roar of rain,
and clouds stay close
but with a hunger,
and the birds are still,
and their stillness
hurts more than their song.

Anything the Landlord Touches

I break things because I am afraid and I spend my time repairing
It's almost the expression of love
I found these beautiful machines abandoned here
Sometimes there is nothing to inherit

It's almost the expression of love
To hunt, to seduce, to deal with a stone
Sometimes there is nothing to inherit
Footprints on the path that leads to the house

To hunt, to seduce, to deal with a stone
I set out, taking my precautions
Footprints on the path that leads to the house
I did not even know that I was naked

I set out, taking my precautions
Out of a desire unclear even to myself
I did not even know that I was naked
The house swaying, it is always empty

Out of a desire unclear even to myself
I found these beautiful machines abandoned here
The house swaying, it is always empty
I break things because I am afraid and I spend my time repairing

Pali

Flourish the little flower in the lemon-coloured hands
A grown child is known to be sorrow
Not crumpled, like the meagre of the town
These lines have been preserved, and I have read them

A grown child is known to be sorrow
Our words, and our becoming what we tame
These lines have been preserved, and I have read them
A snarl of him grows in me

Our words, and our becoming what we tame
The Wild Boy never spoke, the Wild Boy was abandoned
A snarl of him grows in me
But still there is some hope in a light place

The Wild Boy never spoke, the Wild Boy was abandoned
The Wild Boy was put in a house and forgotten
But still there is some hope in a light place
The doorway is himself, woven with want

The Wild Boy was put in a house and forgotten
Not crumpled, like the meagre of the town
The doorway is himself, woven with want
Flourish the little flower in the lemon-coloured hands

Poem

Decaying thunder,
all the ordinary rain.
A raft of tiny fools,
a poem of nails.

New Poems

A Crushing Spring

People pity me for marrying a blind man,
but I possess a small oval face.
We travel in the carriage with the ordinary passengers.
Switzerland, so the water is very clean.

We never speak of his disease, only of his new beliefs.
The house is large and beautiful.
Felled trees lead to memories, infinitely gentle and unfelt.
Imagine me with strange servants.

I behave like an angel when he stumbles in the garden.
The summerhouse is on fire.
Do you see how it is, how I am bound here?
I feel so perfectly sure the final blow has been struck.

Seven Days to Apologise

Most-watched,
I like your work:
It tortures, flinches, fleeces.
I'm needy, I'll pay –
Sell out to me.

Shaman, convention, stencil –
I'm all three.
Soon I'll be my real self,
Not my holiday self.
And I'll tell you my real name.

Love was always confused
With sport and soap.
Now love is making me want
To treat your lisp,
Localise the pain.

Those famous people dropping in:
'My yacht ran aground
In the mouth of the channel.
May I use your phone?'
You've been in on the fraud

and I can't let it pass.
Just don't say the mood is doomed:
Aeroplanes are doomed.
What prescription can I fill
to leave you frailer?

Tainted Version

I'm hoping for something a little better,
one bright idea to push me over the edge.
How come I don't see love in your eyes when you look at me?
Why did I have to find out about it second-hand?

The cracks in the mirror,
that's very poetic.
I mean, could you sleep?
Could your soul rest?
Actually it would be preferable if you vanished into thin air.
I've got my hands full just hanging by a thread.

Think about what I said,
you're hurt and you're angry.
That's how it should be,
how it has to be.
You'd better smile because animals can sense fear in a person.
I'm back from the dead,
you should be overjoyed.

Detail for a Lily Scheme

When a woman gets married it is because she is hungry, thirsty
    or naked.
Take her straight from the fields and threshing floors.
Her silence means consent.
Give her anything, so long as it's gold.

Not strong or pure or beautiful,
she simmers like a bone in soup,
so that all you can hold against her is her silence.
You'll think it's piety wasting her.

Desperate and meaningless words, why would she utter them?
The habits of serfdom seem to die hard.
Never let her get her hands on the contents of your cabinets.
It's autumn already. Can the forest burn?

Arraignment Song

The same show every time – that's death
Flash boat, fast cars – it's all going to end
Go cosy, slow, investigate
Dead ten years when the letter was mailed

Flash boats, fast cars – it's all going to end
Assume a certain monkey wrench
Dead ten years when the letter was mailed
Nice clothes, expensive dental work

Assume a certain monkey wrench
Blood pooling poetically around the fingers
Nice clothes, expensive dental work
Tropical fish and some books on the subject

Blood pooling poetically around the fingers
Back where you started with the bitter pills
Tropical fish and some books on the subject
Psychos like to work together

Back where you started with the bitter pills
Everyone has solid alibis
Psychos like to work together
Stop on one thought, think it over and over

Everyone has solid alibis
So listen and record the names
Stop on one thought, think it over and over
Who faked a will, didn't mourn the loss?

So listen and record the names
No one wants to sit with frailty
Who faked a will, didn't mourn the loss?
In spring killers get jittery

No one wants to sit with frailty
A lit cigarette at a respectful distance
In spring killers get jittery
If the family find peace, disturb it

A lit cigarette at a respectful distance
Slim chance connects you to a name
If the family find peace, disturb it
Night's your office, shadowing pays

Slim chance connects you to a name
Go cosy, slow, investigate
Night's your office, shadowing pays
The same show every time – that's death

Rattling the Forms

I wanted to dissolve my marriage, explode the limits,
seek comfort, oblivion, anything in caves,
on a whaling ship, in a hundred other places.

Shrewd reverie in my perilous head,
I struck out through the shambling waves:
I wanted to dissolve my marriage, explode the limits!

Beyond waterfalls and time lost and the first chastities to mar
    the shore,
defenceless men set me aflame,
on a whaling ship, in a hundred other places.

Not me at all, but my double, my look-alike;
not someone but anyone in a sort of cloak and hood –
I wanted to dissolve my marriage, explode the limits.

I *am* a kind of guillotine! I am *not* unlimited sorrow!
How bare the narrative seems! And nothing! And nothing
    and nothing and nothing…
on a whaling ship, in a hundred other places!

If you could only see me riding on and on,
babbling like a saint in the open fields!
I wanted to dissolve my marriage, explode the limits,
on a whaling ship, in a hundred other places.

Newborn

'Falling fiery worm,
poor thirsty mortal,

secretive dreamboat
with sniper eyes,

mouth open
for impossible mercy:

monsoon in the cradle,
who are you?'

—

'A more slippery beauty,
my own father is haunted.

Maybe I'm wrenlike –
busy with wreaths.

I steal deeper sleep,
what drives me is sensual.

The gods are with me
and I'm going to win!'

Fragile Pranks

I left anyway, in spirit
dreamed I was living my own life
my mind was on exits, I tried to buy the truth
some nights until I ran out of dark

dreamed I was living my own life
started strange, went familiar
some nights until I ran out of dark
falling into the depths of whatever

started strange, went familiar
I survived so many banishments
falling into the depths of whatever
I woke up in the camp of the assassins

I survived so many banishments
dissolving myself in the arms of third parties
I woke up in the camp of the assassins
the kleptomaniacs, never more beautiful

dissolving myself in the arms of third parties
that was when I felt closest to god
the kleptomaniacs, never more beautiful
the deal fell through but the point was made

that was when I felt closest to god
my mind was on exits, I tried to buy the truth
the deal fell through but the point was made
I left anyway, in spirit

Precursors

O NEVSKY CROWDS filling Katherine's Hall like a veil
streaming past the sentry boxes and the porters' lodges
as if having agreed on an exact time and place by telegraph...

and YOU
mercenaries and half-virtuous women
torch-bearers
exiles
poets of peasant origins
orphans (more like old dwarfs than children)...

ALL singing horribly...

looking
but not seeing
like rain...

as if in blind acceptance of fate
unaccountably godless...

so that in the end
frantic
you almost forget the existence of the sun...

(which condition can only lead to the gallows
as anyone who reads the chronicles of events will tell you)

after all
you are human
you might live or you might destroy...

a hundred times
before morning...

when wrath gives way to kindness and you laugh like lunatics
alarming the city's famished cats!

Far from the Pearly Shell

When a woman wishes to be cruel,
she is more cruel.
Her gestures are always accompanied by winter winds,
so that now her eyes seem even more beautiful and tragic.
Such is the clarity of her rare destiny,
that she wakes at dawn and boards a train,
without explanation,
to come south.
Imagine someone dangerous and diseased;
silent, despite dark clothing.
She should never have been allowed past
the convent doors.
Marry her and you marry disquiet.

Freight

That's the path we would have
taken, there were many like us,
like a shadow on the lung,
and it didn't cost the earth,
after all. Relocated to the east
in autumn, but is that so important?
The crowded rooms, the fabric
much too thin for the time of year.
Yes, stripped of all that is human
where the roads abandon their
villages. Remember: everything is
transitory, even the disturbances;
even the sunlight, trees and fields.

That's how long we shouted.
The silence is the silence.
The child spies on the mother,
day pays for night. Freight trains
will arrive at their destinations.
The forest runs along the border,
we must not forget that. And
the moon is in the heavens,
fighting to get free when held.

Speculative Realms

How stupid of me to forget what I really came for!
I came to mourn my stage lover.
A revolutionary and a thinker,
he swallowed gold and died, but died light –

his limbs were merely loosed from the principle of life.
I see them in motion as an engineer sees masses and systems,
or as we observe octopuses and anemones in the sea.
I am with child and hope soon to miscarry.

One day I received a gift of silk and brocade;
the next a sumptuous banquet –
until I lost my bearings completely,
fell ill and suffered great depression.

And I came to compose an essay on the function of sacrifice,
on the primitive forms of classification,
and to learn if we belong to others and not to ourselves,
for the path of liberation is mad and hard and long.

The future evolves in the absence of meaning,
the will of the masses, the lowering and lifting.
Chaos persists and leads to inner haunting,
spreading ruinously, as in dreams.

So I'll go on suffering with a kind of relish
in the shadow of heroic virtues,
until my errors of allegiance are forgotten
or I fall into a brook one morning, very simple!

Poem

Adultery fucks a family up as much as poverty
Because the memories can't run away from home
That's a lot of hatred from a mother
Nothing I'd care to discuss right now

Because the memories can't run away from home
Once a kid learns guilt he's going to stumble
Nothing I'd care to discuss right now
Never grew any taller, just sadder and angrier

Once a kid learns guilt he's going to stumble
I quit school to escape the staring eyes
Never grew any taller, just sadder and angrier
I know that nobody ever changed history, but I had to try

I quit school to escape the staring eyes
The sun, the silence, the nothingness
I know that nobody ever changed history, but I had to try
Part of what makes me interesting for science

The sun, the silence, the nothingness
It was like an acid eating into me
Part of what makes me interesting for science
You're beautiful. What's the emergency?

It was like an acid eating into me
No sexual act ever commenced, instead I trashed the room
You're beautiful. What's the emergency?
Everyone's got their own version of the truth

No sexual act ever commenced, instead I trashed the room
Just want to see if property feels pain
Everyone's got their own version of the truth
Maybe some day, but not today

Just want to see if property feels pain
It's going to end in infinity, and if there is no infinity
Maybe some day, but not today
Can't stop love from doing its damage

It's going to end in infinity, and if there is no infinity
That's a lot of hatred from a mother
Can't stop love from doing its damage
Adultery fucks a family up as much as poverty

Luminous Alias

The strangeness will wear off

JACKSON POLLOCK

You passed out, you don't understand.
Those years were stolen from me.
I think I made friends with the slobs of Hollywood and perished out there.
I travel light, but this is too light.

I *was* conscious, like a child-bride.
I lived in their villas, ricocheted through the halls of fame,
radiating love, going for the jugular.
Wound up further away than anyone.

There's a lot of mystery in the world,
stuff I never read in languages I don't speak.
Saddest circus I ever saw.
I do crave love, but is this the place?

I'm sorry if I added darkness,
but I couldn't just show up empty-handed.
Time to cut and run. It's a sensitive subject.
Even the rain is black. Is everybody helpless here?

Keep your eyes on the road, that's a kind of kissing.
We're bound for nowhere, it's a beautiful place –
somewhere between serenity and vertigo.
I'm grown up. Allow me to show you.

Long primrose nights are coming back to haunt me.
I know that's my life flashing up there on the screen.
I travel light, but this is too light.
Enough of the games. Tell me what I already know.

Ghetto Poem

The spectacle is not so chilling after all.
By degrees the people become accustomed to the gate,
to the work, to the little injustices.
Still others find relief in poetry.
Anyone may stumble all of a sudden.
Trust is a laudable virtue only in ordinary times.
With awe and reverence, I am hiding
the pages that can tell about the quiet groans.
I have trifled with the fear of death,
the shameful recoiling and desire to strike.
But can one wear the clothes of someone who has perished?
Can one eat in the presence of a corpse?

Portion

I was a translucent child.
Nothing could cure me of the folly of ringing the bells whenever
    it thundered,
especially in the hours before dawn.
The sea was fragile then, or so it seemed to me.

The only visitors we had were eagles,
and poor Elisabeth the horse.
All our servants left at the first rumour of war.
I wore dark cloud, I washed with strong soap.

It's like tapestry, time passes,
as slowly as possible, in waves until nightfall.
If my mother had lived, I would have asked about her lovers.
It's better she went, she'd have disgraced us.

I have stopped reading Byron because it was burning me.
O I go to church, I go to church.
And after that I bathe in salt air,
as any disfigured young woman would do.

No one, just myself and the shadow of my father,
his drinking and his infinities,
his ravings about who is and who is not a heretic.
'Fortune' is a strange word I cannot quite fathom.

Pangs

It's my turn to enter the realm of beauty,
to be ground into a flickering light.
I've had to suppress my emotions and rely on reason alone.
Evening prayer tears my gown.
And I don't know when I will be able to rest
with pious whispers under your hands.
But none of this matters now because I want to lay bare my soul:
black, black, black, black, black.

Everything is flowering strangely.
I love you, I must see you again, but I can't be tied down.
For weeks I've been in commotion, turning my brain, and about what?
Disjointed thoughts which I've brought with me from the great valleys of the sea,
and a letter, probably from a madman, stating that I am certain to become very rich,
and some of the exquisite pain of early spring…

Forgive me and have pity on me and send a present.
No gardener in his senses blames a rose.
I crossed Paris like a meteor. In Vienna I regained composure,
but all this time I've felt quite odd, as if I couldn't do anything right.
I doubt I could even shoot a bird with an arrow,
and Robert tells me that the glorious fresh air of his father's farm,
the birch trees, the clear skies,
would only confuse me.

Damn those who said that I was loafing in the city!
My last pennies are spent and I'm suffering the pangs.
It's as if I'm only half-existing, like the shadow of the pyramids.
I'll try to explain, even though I don't really understand it myself.
There's too much 'Scythian' uproar, too much sounding of alarms.
All the symptoms of all the disorders
come and go in a continual stream…I am enchanted…

Kanipshins

In consideration for my mother,
the yacht got free of its moorings.
'Just bring him home:
I'll decide who's handsome.'
We tried to quarrel quietly in the bathroom.
She had kept certain phrases for this moment
but ended up expressing desperation
through the elaborateness
of her hairdo, and drama,
the way she salted her food.

'So the daughter empties the mother!'
(Bejewelled, knitting at top speed,
on the sofa with strength fading,
briefly distracted by new plaid.)
'He's youngish, tall ... he's Jewish –
you should be falling all over him!'
Some things can only be said
in a lavish dressing gown.

'*And* he's got beautiful manners...
From the day you were born,
I've been planning your wedding.'
The drug companies did the serenading,
but how the girdle must have hurt!

All that mystery about germs,
the earthshaking
finale of her scenes,
holding lilies, almost apoplectic.
Funny and stupid,
like us dressing up as twins.

Finishing School

I know that my pupil is imperfect.
It may be that herein lies her strength.
Small hands, soft sighs – evidence of a passionate nature.
Sure enough, the foot is deformed.

Her eyes are deep, like ponds of black water.
She knows very well how to burrow in the darkness.
It is bitterness I want to teach her –
of which life is woven, the wild bible.

Sweet dreams, delusive hopes.
The taint is passed on from mother to child.
How could anyone as pale as she, I wonder, sit so silently?
I'll never tire of punishing her.

Needles of Gauges

Yesterday I fashioned mirrors of thin ebonite.
I hammered out the flaws as morning broke,
fogging the surfaces like incurable rage,
filling my laboratory with visions.

I tested first on densities of glass
for the intervention of air and earth
between the axle and the frame,
between the shaft and the cog that turns,
and the distances were warm with thought
in four sections of the spherical casing.

All day, my proofs, gouged into paper,
accumulated like silent tides:
'Persistence of what is softest of all.'
'Prussic acid, because it seems to slow light down.'
'Translucency is just the moment of holding.'

My mind was very dark,
weighted with fragments –
time, matter, all elements of being.
And then the sighting of certain constellations,
and then actually dreaming,
rising out of the collar of my coat.

Sugared Path

Thanks for coming by so late in such a beautiful
state of mind. The stars dream this way. We
can't keep running from the past. The stones
on the road: like I said, it's just a hunch. You
won't be smiling much longer because I'm starting
to remember things about my life.
                                                    Relax, it's not
what you're thinking. You saved my life, you
nursed me back to health. First day of spring.
Let's face it: you screwed up. I find myself trying
to believe in the void and it's got me a little
confused.
              This is a city of terrible fire. That's
the problem. I've got you to hold onto. It's not
the life I would have chosen, so keep the air off
of me. History's still in rough shape, I guess that
answers my question.
                                        Truth, love and happiness,
that's the direction I'm headed. Look at the facts:
I'm supposed to be a fountain of tears. We're
back where we started, the darkest part of
the whole garden, and that's the past sitting right
over there. There's a tidal wave coming, I just
always assumed.

It's a one in a million chance, but it's possible. I'm talking about you lighting up like a storm. I could have accepted your gift, but I'm wiser, I've learned from my mistakes. I'd sign anything for daylight again.

Avalanches

I travelled like a curse
hunting when the ice was moving
my hands, for once, staying still, not stealing
but I saw what I was doing, and seeing it broke down my silence

hunting when the ice was moving
not just any stranger pushing her own decay
but I saw what I was doing, and seeing it broke down my silence
I saw it all, the wolves howling

not just any stranger pushing her own decay
still trembling like the sun
I saw it all, the wolves howling
dividing the remnant again and again

still trembling like the sun
and me, deep in debt when the great pine trees began to fall
dividing the remnant again and again
my beautiful army had been destroyed

and me, deep in debt when the great pine trees began to fall
where was I in the storm, leaving the broken glass on the ground
    and the hammer in its midst?
my beautiful army had been destroyed
yesterday, when I wanted the winter to close over me

where was I in the storm, leaving the broken glass on the ground
    and the hammer in its midst?
the spears of winter found my hands
yesterday, when I wanted the winter to close over me
how could I, being compass-less?

the spears of winter found my hands
my hands, for once, staying still, not stealing
how could they, being compass-less?
I travelled like a curse

Poker for Money

It's not the blank stare
of another sucker or
the close shaves I give
much thought to in
the face of such silent
gods. Each day doles
out pieces of the small,
elegant, blue testimony,
deepening my aliases,
in the manner of
whomever I'm with.
It rains, it doesn't rain.

See? I could smother
you right now…and then
I let you go. I'm gunpowder,
beginning in shreds with
some boys in
the neighbourhood
to stay afloat. Just like
that (snap of the fingers)
I'm gone again, with
the keys to the kingdom.
Borrowed time's
such a beautiful gift.

But it's always a case
of the right illusion;
say, twenty more than
your body language.
Like a chef and his
sauce, my precious
winning hand. Very
docile, very nice:
that's how I remain
on the face of the earth,
like finding a stray dog
and bringing it home.

Loose in the fact of
death, I'm obeying
nobody, taking roads
almost nowhere,
menacing decorous
little worlds. It won't
be in a rabbit suit, but
I'll come quietly
down in the morning,
when the jackpot's
paying out its salt
and words.

Lesson

At first I did not have enough resoluteness.
I was a woman who only quarrelled and was a burden to people,
or sat quietly and never spoke up during meetings – that's not proper.
I had the attitude, 'You can talk as much as you want, but it's all
 the same, nothing will come of it.'
At that time I could not reason sensibly.
Then, in the spring, in May of this year,
a brigade of soldiers came to us,
and my head began to clear.
I realised that I was wrong to behave as I had done, and I promised
 to try to remedy my deficiencies.
I stood up and recounted my whole life and all my crimes.
In forthright language I denounced drunkenness and the corruption
 of public morals.
I said that the rye had been threshed extremely poorly,
that so many of our tools were broken and lay about anywhere,
that fire had burned down the barn containing felt boots and galoshes,
all because of saboteurs, underminers and self-willed people,
and I called for them to be deported out of the bounds of the village.
I concluded in a very slow and clear manner,
so as to assist the person whose job it is to write everything down
 and make a report,
'The death of the Red Army man should remain in our memories all our
 lives as a lesson:
If the horse drowns,
proceed on foot.'

Acknowledgements

Several poems in the 'New' section first appeared in the chapbook *Luminous Alias* as part of Vagabond Press's Rare Objects series. Other poems from this section have appeared in *Australian Poetry Since 1788*, *Cordite Poetry Review* and in multiple volumes of *The Best Australian Poetry* anthology. My thanks to the editors.

The Giramondo Publishing Company acknowledges the support of Western Sydney University in the implementation of its book publishing program.

This project has been assisted by the Commonwealth Government through the Australia Council, its arts funding and advisory body.